DISCARDED

DISCARDED

Cresson Public Library

Believe it or Not Space Facts

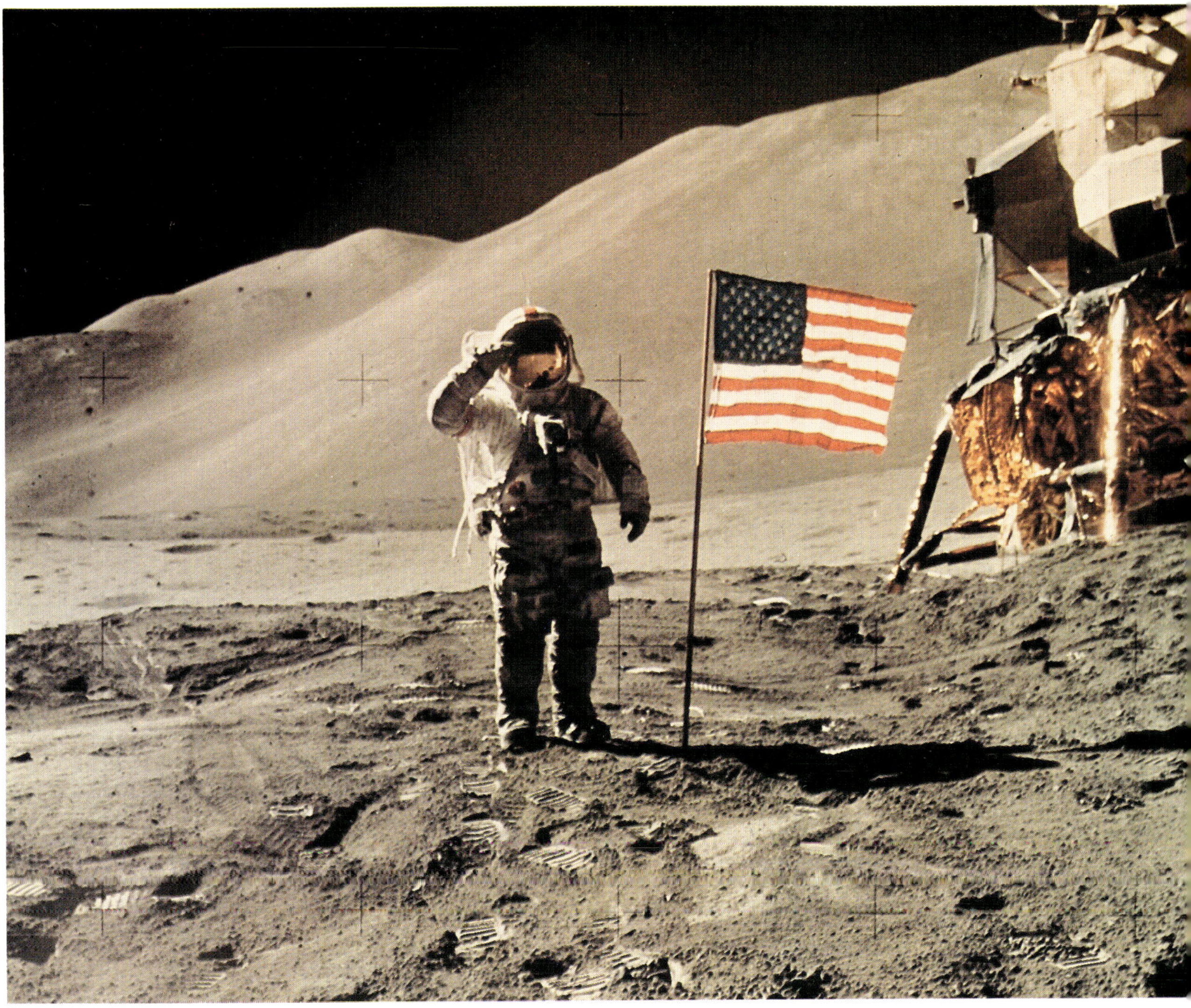

Today's World in Space

Believe it or Not Space Facts

By David Baker

Rourke Enterprises, Inc.
Vero Beach, FL 32964

© 1988 Rourke Enterprises, Inc.

All rights reserved. No part of this book may be reproduced or utilized in any form or by any means, electronic or mechanical including photocopying, recording or by any information storage and retrieval system without permission in writing from the publisher.

Library of Congress Cataloging-in-Publication Data

Baker, David, 1944-
  Believe it or not—space facts / David L. Baker.

  p. cm. — (Today's world in space)
  Bibliography: p.
  Includes index.
  Summary: Elaborates on forty facts about astronautics, outer space, and astronomy, from the technique used to take a shower in space to the behavior of falling objects in a vacuum.
    1. Astronautics—Juvenile literature.
2. Astronomy—Juvenile literature. [1. Astronautics.
2. Outer Space. 3. Astronomy.] I. Title. II. Series:
Baker, David, 1944-   . Today's world in space.
TL793.B234 1987   500.5--dc19   87-19890
ISBN 0-86592-407-4   CIP
                                                AC

CONTENTS

Space Facts   6

    40 scientific facts about rockets, satellites, the galaxy, and space travel.

Glossary   46

Index   47

The biggest rocket engine ever built generates almost half the power produced by all the moving water in North America.

In March, 1926, Robert Goddard was the first person to fire a liquid propellant rocket into the air. For many years only small rockets were possible. By the late 1950s, work began on a very big rocket motor called the F-1. It was designed to power the mighty Saturn V rocket which would launch men to the moon between 1969 and 1972. The F-1 produced 750 tons of thrust, more than ten times the power of the biggest engine then built. Each F-1 was 19 feet tall, 12 feet 4 inches wide across the big exhaust cone, consumed nearly 3 tons of fuel a second, and weighed more than 9 tons. The F-1 was built by Rocketdyne at their plant in California. Five F-1 engines powered the first stage of the Saturn V. Together, they burned more than 2,200 tons of fuel in 2 minutes and 30 seconds. They produced 3,750 tons of thrust to push the second and third stages to a speed of 6,000 MPH and a height of 38 miles.

The biggest rocket engine ever built was designed for the Saturn V moon rocket, and produced thrust of 750 tons.

Rockets work better in a vacuum. Why?

A rocket works by producing a stream of particles in a fixed direction at high speed. The 18th-century scientist Isaac Newton said that every action brings an equal and opposite reaction. The rocket works because the exhaust produces a motion in one direction, propelling the rocket in the exact opposite direction. Many forces in the atmosphere play on the rocket to reduce its efficiency. At sea level, air squeezes in upon every square inch with a pressure of nearly 15 pounds. This force slows the speed of the particles rushing through the exhaust nozzle. Because the speed of the rocket depends upon the speed of the exhaust, air pressure causes a reduced efficiency. Also, air pressing on the front of the rocket itself is a force that must be overcome. Each second the rocket climbs up through the atmosphere, it is becoming more and more efficient. In a *vacuum,* or empty space, the rocket is at its most efficient.

Rocket motors operating in the atmosphere are at a handicap because of the pressure of the air. They are more efficient in a vacuum.

More energy is required to reach orbit from Earth than to go from earth orbit to the planet Mars.

We all live at the bottom of a well — a gravity well. Just outside the earth's atmosphere is a region from which trips to the moon and the planets can be made much more easily. A spacecraft must be pushed from zero to 17,500 MPH just to get to earth orbit 150 miles up. From there it takes just a 9,200 MPH push to travel *250,000 miles* to moon orbit. From moon orbit, a spacecraft needs just a 1,500-MPH reduction in speed to land on the surface, because the moon has only one-sixth the gravity of earth. Scientists believe that a space station orbiting the earth is the best place from which to build and launch probes to the moon and other places in the solar system. From earth orbit, a space vehicle needs just a 12,000 MPH shove to head off for Mars. At Mars, a speed cut of just 3,600 MPH will drop it into orbit. For these reasons, NASA wants to build a station in space and begin sending expeditions out to explore the solar system.

A huge amount of energy is required to reach earth orbit. Rockets must be very powerful to overcome the strong pull of gravity close to the earth's surface.

The shuttle weighs more than a U.S. Navy warship.

The shuttle consists of three main parts. The orbiter has wings and flies like an airplane to come back down through the atmosphere and land on a runway. It weighs about 85 tons and can carry 30 tons of cargo, up to a maximum combined weight of 115 tons. Its three engines are fed from oxygen and hydrogen carried in the big external tank. This tank weighs 33 tons empty and contains 795 tons of propellant, for a total weight of 828 tons. The two big solid rocket boosters each weigh 90 tons empty and 645 tons when fueled. On the pad, the loaded shuttle weighs 2,233 tons. The two boosters are separated at 2 minutes after launch and jettisoned, which reduces the shuttle's weight by 1,290 tons. By this time, the shuttle has consumed about 200 tons of liquid fuel from the external tank, and as it continues to use fuel, its weight is reduced to about 150 tons before the tank is released. When the tank is dumped, the shuttle weighs about 115 tons, only five percent of its weight on the launch pad.

Below: When the orbiter lands back on Earth, it weighs around 100 tons, although it can land with up to 15 tons in its cargo bay.

Above: When the shuttle takes off from the launch pad at Cape Canaveral, it weighs more than 2,200 tons. It sheds most of this weight in the first eight minutes after launch.

Taking a shower in space is tricky because water cannot flow in weightlessness.

Weightlessness is one of the most enjoyable things about space travel. Any astronaut will tell you that. But there are problems. Nothing behaves quite the same as it does on the earth's surface. The very act of removing the influence of gravity changes most things. Washing or taking a shower becomes a real problem. Water separates into globules and floats about. It will not flow as it does under the influence of gravity. Without the presence of gravity, surface tension takes over as the dominant force. Surface tension occurs because a group of molecules resist change. In space, the water molecules cling together. Try gently tipping a cup of water until it almost flows over the rim. The water resists the flow and surface tension holds it until gravity overwhelms the resistance. Astronauts use a special kind of spray jet to shower in space. They use a special vacuum to mop up the floating globules afterward.

Skylab astronaut Pete Conrad takes a shower aboard the orbiting space station.

A fire in a spacecraft would probably put itself out.

Some people have phobias, or fears, of certain things. One fear shared by all astronauts is that a fire might start in their spacecraft. The shuttle is built with many fire ports around the cabin. In each of these ports, the flexible nozzle of a special fire extinguisher can be inserted. The fire extinguisher squeezes a special chemical behind the panels and display consoles to put out hidden fires. An elaborate warning system exists to tell the crew when a fire starts anywhere in the spacecraft. If a fire started in the open cabin, it would probably put itself out, because there is no convection in weightlessness. Just as there is no force pulling everything toward the floor, there is no way heat can rise. Smoke produced by fire would smother the flames and leave no oxygen to keep it burning. Scientists believe that the absence of convection will enable them to produce new and better alloys in space, because they will cool down evenly.

Above: The many panels aboard the Shuttle orbiter have tiny ports through which foam can be squeezed to put out fires that might start in hidden electrical equipment.

Below: Much of the equipment inside the shuttle could malfunction and cause a fire, so precautions are very important.

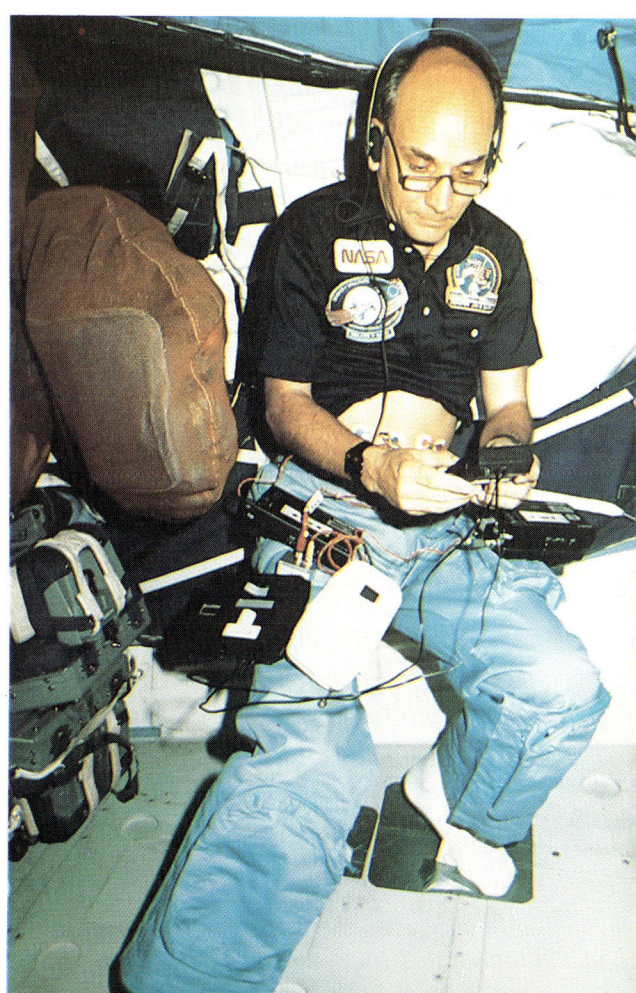

Plants grow upside down in space.

Space scientists have always been interested to discover the effects of weightlessness on many different things. Since the space program began, satellites have carried many living things into orbit. The effect of weightlessness on humans has been well documented. The effect on plants and food concerns scientists, because people might need to grow their own vegetables in space one day. Several experiments aboard orbiting laboratories have shown what happens to plants in weightlessness. Unlike plants on earth, plants grown in space follow the brightest light. In space there is no recognized presence of gravity. The plants do not know which direction is up and which is down. This seems to make little difference to their roots. Plant roots continue to grow out from the bottom of the stem just as they do on Earth. Some plants grow better in space and others grow more quickly. Most produce more leaves and better seeds.

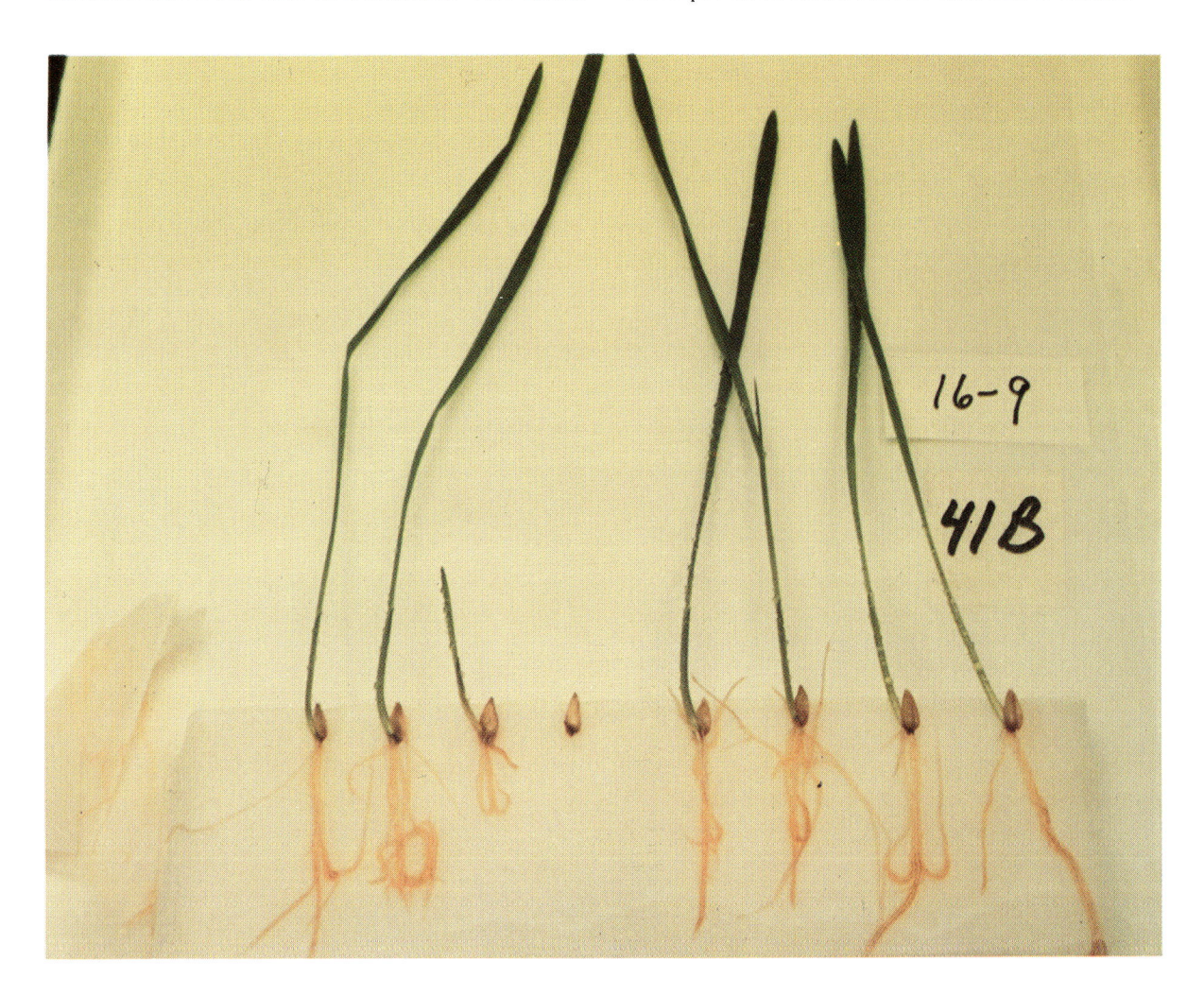

These pine cone seedlings were grown in space aboard a NASA shuttle mission in 1984 and were shown to be healthy and strong.

On long space flights the bones of a weightless astronaut could become brittle and break.

When astronauts first went into space, no one knew what effect weightlessness would have on the human body. Many people feared that astronauts would be affected by radiation from the sun. Other people thought the crushing effect of rocket power would damage their bones. The real effects were not predicted. When people spend long periods of time in space, their bones lose calcium. Bones are living things and not merely a frame for our body. Bones need regular supplies of calcium and other minerals to keep them healthy and alive. Very long space flights have shown that if astronauts remained weightless for two years, their bones would become brittle. Astronauts in this condition might not be able to return to Earth, because their bones could no longer support their body weight in a gravity situation. They would become the first space humanoids, condemned to weightlessness for ever.

Astronauts carry out medical experiments in space to measure the effects of weightlessness on their bodies.

Experiments show that drugs can be produced better in space than on Earth.

Tests conducted aboard the NASA shuttle have shown that some drugs can be made more efficiently in space. Weightlessness encourages a process called *electrophoresis,* which is vital to the production of important drugs and medicines. Every biological and chemical susbstance has an electric charge. In electrophoresis, a mixture of substances is placed in a chamber filled with a fluid. The chamber is given an electrical field and the substances separate according to their charge. This gives scientists pure samples to make drugs from. On Earth, gravity makes it difficult to prepare some complicated medicines. In weightless space, the effects of gravity are not felt. Over 700 times more material, four times purer than earth samples, can be prepared in space. Tests have been carried out on seven shuttle missions, and a production unit will be set up in orbit during the 1990s.

Astronaut Charles Walker works on an experiment aimed at producing better drugs and medicines for sick people on earth.

Pictures from space reveal details the human eye would never see.

Pictures from space reveal details the human eye would never see.

When the first astronauts went into space, they saw things on the ground they never expected to find. The view from orbit, just 150 miles above the surface, revealed details impossible to predict. Scientists built satellites to monitor the earth and take advantage of this view. Because satellites orbit the earth every 90 minutes or so, one satellite can monitor a wide area. The satellites carry special cameras to photograph features the human eye cannot see. All light comes from different bands in a *spectrum* of colors from red to violet. Colors outside that spectrum are said to be *infrared* or *ultraviolet,* but the eye cannot see them. Infrared colors indicate small changes in temperature. Infrared cameras on satellites can reveal different rocks, soils, minerals, and crops. View from satellites also show the health of crops and detect diseases before farmers can detect them by inspection.

Above: The view from space is surprisingly good, and many objects can be seen.

Below: Special cameras are used to take pictures in areas of the spectrum that the human eye cannot see, revealing features visible to humans for the first time.

Some satellites will orbit the earth for millions of years.

Some satellites will orbit the earth for millions of years.

The first United States satellite, *Explorer 1,* was launched from Cape Canaveral on January 31, 1958. It was put in an elliptical orbit 221 miles high at the low point and 1,583 miles at the high point. The satellite lasted just over 22 years and fell through the atmosphere on March 31, 1970. The earth's atmosphere extends many thousands of miles into space. Tiny particles of air bumped against the satellite and slowed it down over time. A satellite's orbit depends upon its precise speed and position in space. The more it is slowed, the lower it falls, until it reaches the much denser layers. Sunlight can also affect satellites. The sun sends a stream of radioactive particles through space past Earth. These, too, collide with the satellite and push it off course. Some satellites are so high they will stay in orbit for millions of years. The most stable orbits are circular ones more than 300 miles up.

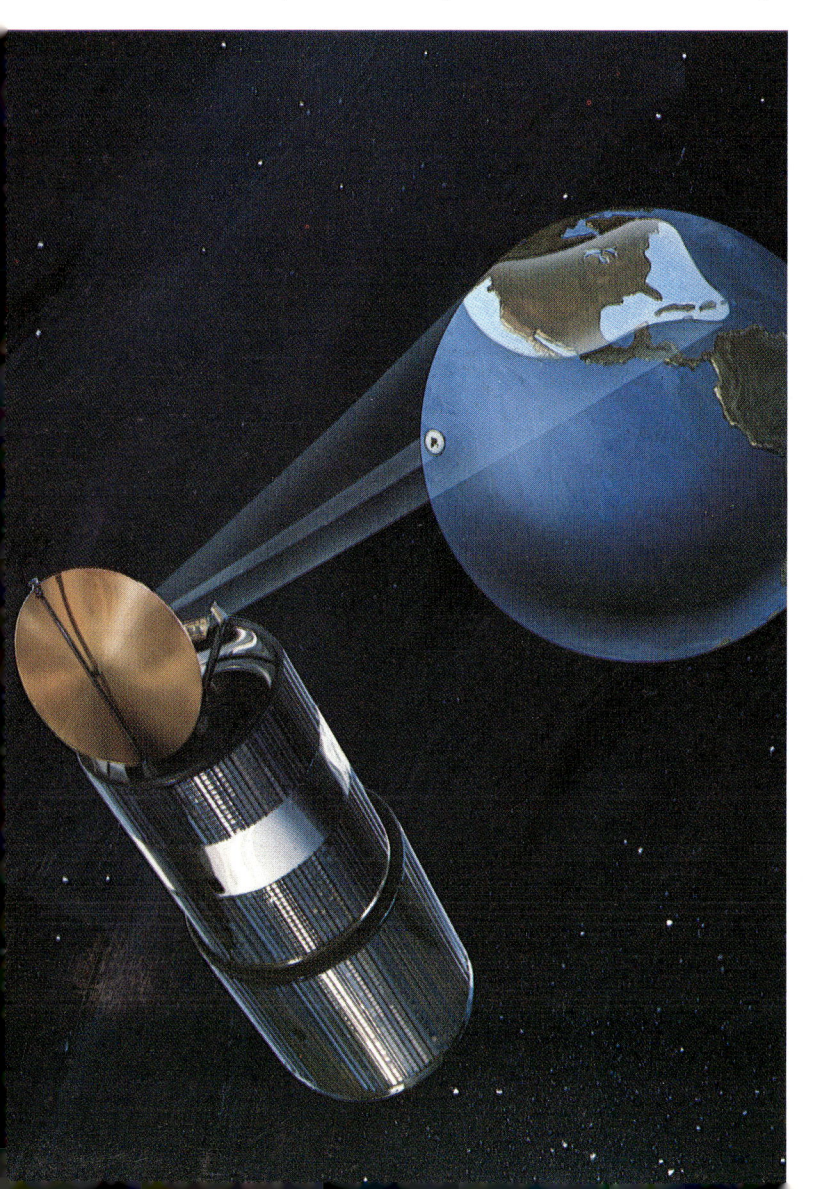

Satellites in very low orbit have a limited lifetime before they spiral back down into the atmosphere. Communications satellites like this one, in stationary orbit 22,000 miles up, will remain in space for millions of years.

A compass would never work in space.

A compass works on Earth because magnetized iron reacts to the earth's magnetic field. There are basically two kinds of *magnetism.* Dipolar magnetism is that which makes all compasses work, because it is the field that makes magnetized metal line up with the earth's magnetic axis. Remanent magnetism is produced when metals and rocks cool down through a certain temperature. The magnetic memory of the earth's dipolar field remains fixed in the metals. When the metals move around they still show the direction of magnetic north. Beyond earth, the magnetic lines trap belts of radiation from the sun. Beyond the radiation belts, each planet has its own magnetic field, smaller or larger than Earth's. The moon has no magnetic field, only remanent magnetism trapped in its rocks when cooled. No space explorer would get far using a compass. With each passing planet, the needle would point in a different direction.

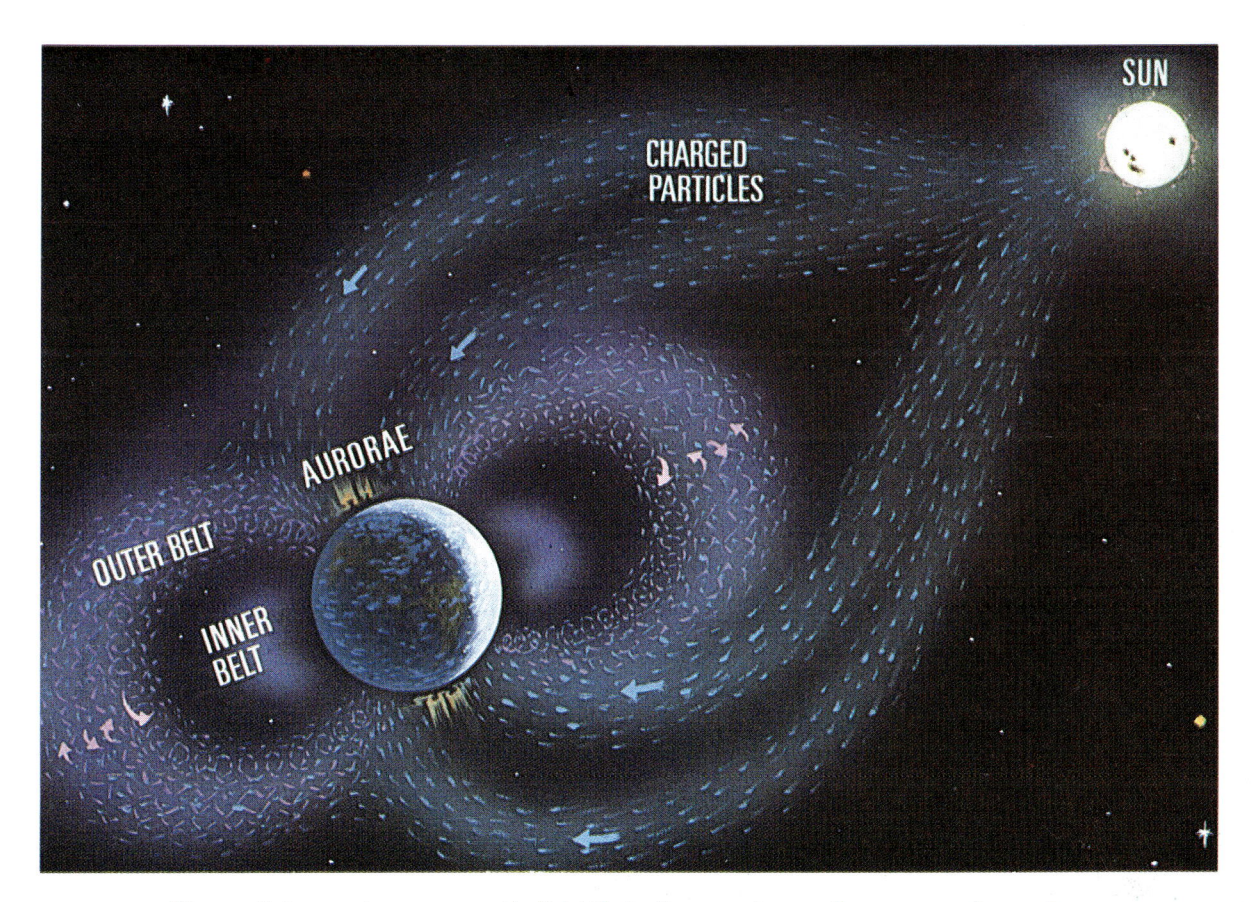

The earth has a strong magnetic field that allows us to use the compass for navigation, but radiation from the sun is trapped in these belts and produces the now familiar magnetosphere around earth.

One day we might get electricity from space.

Almost everything we do uses electrical power. Homes, schools, colleges, universities, research institutes, industry, and government buildings all require electrical power to operate. Most electricity is generated in coal-fired or hydro-electric power stations. Much power is produced in nuclear power stations.

Each method of producing electricity has its drawbacks. Coal pollutes the air, and nuclear reactors produce radioactive waste. Some people think the solution to these problems might be to get our power from space. The sun pours out so much electrical energy each second that if we captured and used only a tiny amount, it could replace every power station on Earth. Engineers have suggested we could build huge stations in space with millions of solar cells. Solar cells convert sunlight into electricity and are used on satellites today. The energy produced could be sent down to Earth on a microwave beam identical to that produced in a microwave oven. The energy would be harmless, free from pollution, and give unlimited amounts of electricity.

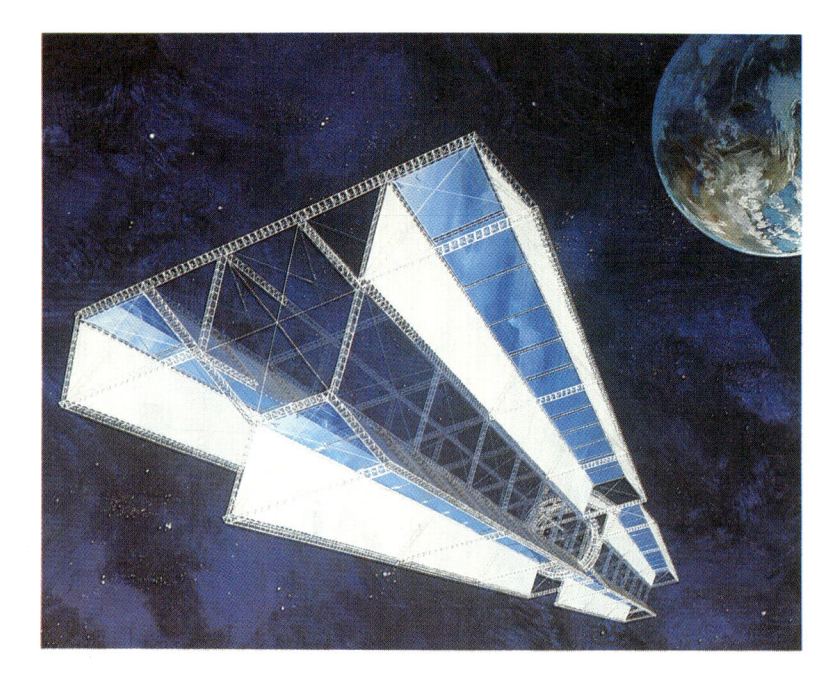

Left: Engineers would like to build a solar power satellite capable of converting sunlight into electricity for people on the ground below.

Right: Electrical energy from solar power satellites would be beamed to the ground as microwave radiation from enormous structures more than twenty miles long.

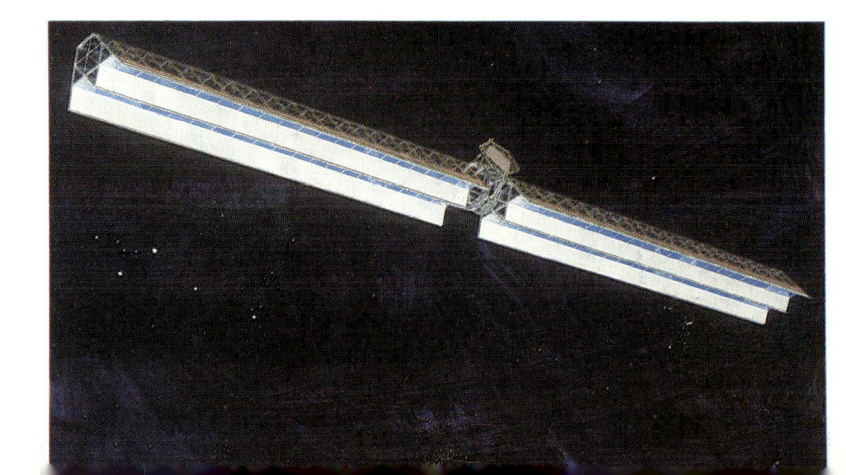

In a vacuum a feather falls as fast as a hammer.

For a long time, people thought that heavy objects fell faster than lighter ones. After all, had anyone ever seen a feather beat a hammer to the ground? Of course not. Yet like to many things in the world around us, our eyes deceive us. What we are really seeing is the pressure of air keeping the feather afloat while the hammer falls like a brick. The 17th-century astronomer Galileo, who invented the telescope, said that all objects fall at the same speed in a vacuum where there is no air to hold things up. Astronauts tried this by dropping a feather and a hammer to the surface of the moon. And guess what? Both objects reached the surface at the same time. This experiment confirmed an important fact: the speed at which any object falls toward another by gravity depends on the mass of the heaviest object. The moon is heavier than either the hammer or feather so they both fall toward its surface at the same rate.

Astronauts on the moon proved that in a vacuum where there is no air, objects of unequal weight will fall at the same speed to the surface.

Robot cameras watched astronauts blast off from the moon.

When the first astronauts went to the moon in July 1969, they carried a TV camera to show moon-watchers on Earth what was happening. It was attached to the side of the lunar module. After stepping onto the moon's surface, the astronauts removed the camera and set it up on a tripod so people could follow their activities. Cameras were also taken on the next two lunar surface missions. On those flights, the astronauts spent several hours away from their landing site. The camera was connected by cable to the *lunar module* and could not be moved away from the landing site. By 1971, a new camera had been built which could be used away from the landing site. The camera was attached to the lunar roving vehicle, a sort of moon buggy. It went everywhere the astronauts went and was remotely controlled from Earth to follow their movements. When the astronauts got back in their lunar module to blast off back to Earth, the camera saw that, too.

The camera on board the Apollo moon rover shot this scene of Apollo 16 igniting its engine to fly back into moon orbit with the two exploring astronauts.

The walls of an Apollo moon lander were so thin you could tear the side open with your hands.

Manned spacecraft like the shuttle are usually built to fly up and down through the atmosphere. They are shaped to avoid being burned up by the friction and designed to fly back to a safe landing. Early spacecraft were shaped like cones. They could not land on runways and splashed down at sea instead. One manned spacecraft was built *never* to survive going either up or down. It was the Apollo lunar module, carried inside a protective shroud on the rocket that launched it. The lower section was left on the moon. There are six lower sections there today, left from the six successful moon visits by Apollo astronauts. The top half carried astronauts from the lunar surface back to the Apollo spacecraft in moon orbit. The pressure cabin that housed the crew was a thick metal cylinder, but all the fuel tanks and systems were fixed outside this. The protective covering that prevented sunlight from overheating all this equipment was so thin you could tear it with your hands.

The frail outer skin of the Apollo lunar module covered fuel tanks, plumbing, and electrical lines to protect it from excess solar heat.

The wheels on NASA's moon car were made using a tool designed by the ancient Egyptians.

When NASA decided to build a moon car, scientists faced some special problems. The moon has no air and lots of dust. A thin tire inflated with air on Earth might explode on the moon. And the moon dust could easily clog and bog down the wheels. Both threats could be dangerous. If astronauts were stranded miles from their lander, they might have difficulty getting back before their oxygen gave out. To make everything safer and prevent moon car wheels getting bogged down, the engineers designed an open mesh wheel. Dust and soil could pass through the mesh and out the other side. The clods of soil would move aside and not bog down the vehicle. When engineers looked for a suitable loom to weave the fine wire mesh, someone suggested an ancient Egyptian loom that seemed just right. It was, and the first moon car had wheels spun on the replica of a loom 4,000 years old.

Above: NASA's moon rover allowed astronauts to roam widely across the lunar surface on three visits in 1971 and 1972.

Below: The moon rover had a camera that could be operated from Earth while the car was driven many miles away from the lunar module, seen here in the distance.

Plants grow better in moon soil than earth soil.

When astronauts went to the moon they spoke of a dead and lifeless world without air, water, or any living thing. Samples of moon rock brought back to Earth helped scientists' understanding of how both Earth and moon had formed more than 4,500 million years ago. To find out more about the chemistry of old moon rocks, scientists carried out special tests and experiments in laboratories all across the nation. One test showed good growing potential for Earth plants. When scientists had satisfied themselves there were no dangerous bugs in lunar samples, they made a miniature moon garden and grew plants and vegetables. Surprisingly, the crops flourished and grew better than expected, even better than those in earth soil. The reason was not hard to find. The moon has a perfect range of the *minerals* and irons that plants and green things need to grow well. Some day, under protective covers, moon dwellers may grow their own food — in moon soil!

Moon soil is a soft, powdery dust which overlays a harder sand-like soil.

We might get steel from the moon one day.

Earth has evolved over billions of years into a dynamic and highly active planet. More than 70 percent of its surface consists of water covering dried lava that forms sea beds and ocean floors. This lava oozes out through giant cracks deep in the ocean and is very thick. The continents are lighter and float on top, getting pushed around like the skin on rice pudding. The moon is different. Because the moon cooled quickly and died, the heavier materials sank to the middle and left a thin skin on top. The moon's crust is about 50 miles thick on the near side and about 80 miles thick on the far side. An abundance of lighter materials, called aluminum silicates, in the crust gives the moon a higher proportion of steel-making elements than Earth has. Someday mining moon dwellers will get their steel from the surface materials lying all around — and export it to Earth.

Moon mining astronauts may one day set up a base to extract rich minerals from materials in the moon's outer crust.

The moon has craters older than life on Earth.

The moon and the planets were formed nearly five billion years ago, when a giant ball of gas and dust collapsed down into a star. The planets and their moons were a by-product of this process. Large clumps of swirling matter welded itself together to form planets. At first the planets were hot, and rivers of boiling rock ran like volcanic eruptions. Rocks and boulders left over from this process collided with the planets. The planets were cooling down. Instead of welding to the molten clumps of material, the rocks and boulders crashed into what were now solid surfaces, creating great basins and craters. The moon received most of its craters between the time it was formed, around 4,500 million years ago, and about 3,000 million years ago. Life first emerged on Earth about 3,500 million years ago. The moon would not have looked much different then, even before life began on Earth.

Moon craters date back several billion years to a time before life emerged on the surface of our earth.

The moon is falling away from the earth, and days are getting longer.

Although scientists do not know exactly when the moon was formed, it probably began when the earth was formed along with the rest of the planets more than 4,500 million years ago. All that time it has been orbiting the earth and probably will in the future. Scientists now believe that the moon is not always going to be the same distance away. Careful measurement of its position in space shows it to be slowly moving away. At present, the moon is about 240,000 miles away and takes just over 27 days to go once around the earth. The earth takes about 24 hours to revolve once on its axis. The moon is slowly moving to a position where it will take 60 days to go once around the earth. The moon exerts a pull on the earth as it does on the oceans to control tides. This will affect our planet and slow it down to a point where the earth will spin once every 60 days. By then the moon will appear to remain fixed over one spot on Earth. Even now the earth is slowing down. But don't worry, you will never be able to notice the difference.

To us, the moon always seems to be the same distance from Earth. Actually it is moving farther and farther away very slowly and will eventually take 60 days to go around the Earth once.

There might be life on Mars after all.

For a long time *astronomers* hoped there was life on Mars. They believed they saw through their telescopes surface features that looked like colonies of people building cities and growing crops. When spacecraft first went there in the 1960s, Mars appeared to be a lifeless world.

Two Viking landers carried experiments to the surface in 1976, looking for signs of life. Scientists held little hope of finding any. The results from tests carried out on soil samples were puzzling. The soil seemed to imitate life, but there were no organisms from dead microbes. Of the four biology experiments, three indicated life but could not produce direct evidence. The fourth was unsure. After more than ten years of trying to reproduce in laboratories what might have been going on at the surface of Mars to give these kind of results, scientists are ready to conclude that simple forms of life might exist there after all.

Above: In 1976 two Viking lander spacecraft descended to the surface of Mars to search for signs of life.

Below: Each Viking lander had a mechanical scoop seen here to the right, used to obtain samples for analysis in the robot's biological instruments.

It probably rained on Mars once, but the latest drought has lasted millions of years.

When spacecraft first went to look at Mars in the mid-1960s, the world they found looked dead. Pictures taken by spacecraft flashing past the planet found craters and jagged mountains, totally unlike the world many had imagined Mars to be. As probes took more pictures and orbited the planet to map the surface, interesting features were revealed. The atmosphere was thin, temperatures very low, and there was little trace of water. When the Viking orbiter looked for landing sites for its lander, it saw some spectacular valleys. From this information, scientists now believe that lakes and seas once covered large areas of Mars and rain storms channeled gulleys across the surface. From orbit, pictures show dried-up river beds, lake beds, stream channels, and rocks dumped by frozen glaciers. Where has this water gone? Probably back down into the crust and into the polar ice caps. Will it ever rain again? Probably not, but no one knows for certain.

Large regions of the surface may have supported water at one point in the history of Mars. One indication of water is this rough part of the surface where an ice glacier once melted.

The sky on Mars really is pink.

On Earth, the sky is blue because light reflected from the water and moisture in the atmosphere makes it so. But have you ever watched a sunset turn the whole sky red? A red sky at night on Earth is caused by dust and grit, lifted into the air by the day's activity. As sunlight cuts through at a low angle, it bends the light into red and rust colors. On Mars that kind of sky is commonplace, because the planet has no free-standing water and reflects all the red colors of rocks and soil. A great amount of dust gets left in the atmosphere, too. Why? Primarily because Mars has two-thirds less gravity than Earth, so bits of dust and grit stay in the atmosphere longer. Also, great winds on Mars circle the planet and whip up storms that last for several weeks, sometimes completely blocking out the sky. The first vivid pictures of a pink Mars sky were taken when Viking landed on the surface in 1976.

As this Viking lander picture shows, the red rust color of the surface is reflected into the thin atmosphere to create a pink sky.

Venus has a surface temperature hot enough to melt lead.

Of all the planets in the solar system, Venus is the closest to Earth. It orbits the sun inside the orbit of the earth. Venus lies about 67 million miles from the sun, whereas Earth lies 93 million miles out. Since astronomers learned Venus was almost identical in size to the earth, they have hoped to find an earth-like world. The truth is very different, as spacecraft found out when they went to explore its atmosphere and surface. Veiled by a dense atmosphere of poisonous carbon dioxide, the atmosphere of Venus behaves like a greenhouse. By trapping certain bands of light, the lower atmosphere heats up to make this the hottest planet in the solar system. At its surface, where atmospheric pressure is nearly one hundred times that at the surface of the earth, the temperature is a staggering 850° F! This temperature is enough to melt lead and several other metals. No life could ever exist on such a hostile world.

No person has seen the surface of Venus, because it is shrouded in thick cloud. Only robot spacecraft have taken a brief glimpse around a limited area.

Some moons are just dirty snowballs.

Look at the moon and it appears to be a solid body like the earth. It is. But some moons are very different. They are not as solid as our moon and seem more like dirty snowballs. In fact they may be just that. When spacecraft visited the multi-moon system around Jupiter and Saturn, they toured moons very different from ours. Close to a giant planet more than 1,300 times the size of Earth, the four largest moons of Jupiter are strange worlds indeed. The strangest, Europa, seems to be made of mud, rock, and ice. Because Europa is close to Jupiter, it is pulled and stretched by gravity from its massive parent. Like tides pulled across the earth's surface by our moon, mud, slush, and ice has been pulled around in Europa's interior. The result is that the moon has become a giant dirty snowball with ice ridges, rock cliffs, and slush marks all across its grubby surface

Above: Most moons of the giant outer planets Jupiter and Saturn are rocky bodies similar to our own moon, with craters and other familiar markings on the surface.

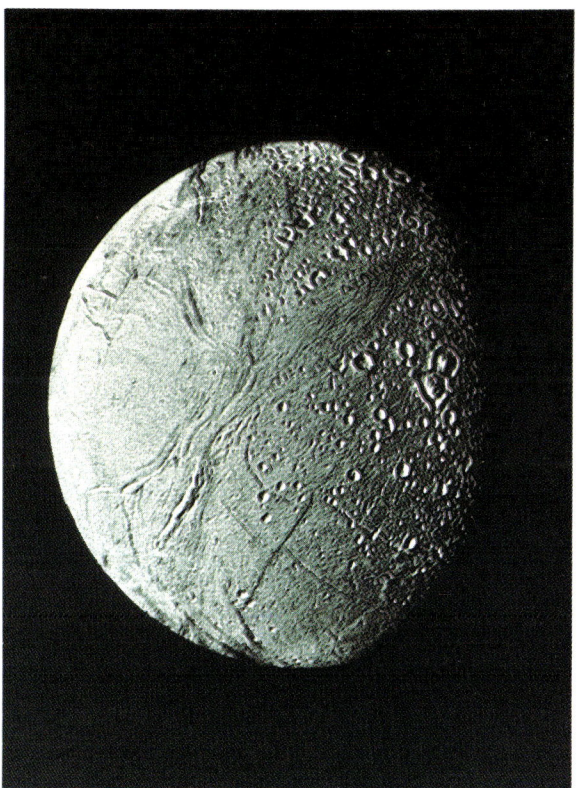

Above: Other moons of the giant planets, however, are much less dense and contain ice and water frozen into cracks and valleys.

Comets are messengers from the past.

Once every 76 years, Halley's Comet comes back from deep space and makes a close pass of the sun. It is one of the most regular visitors in the sky. With their bright long tails like horses' manes, comets have long been associated with disaster and mystery. In reality, they are rocks and boulders left over from the origin of the solar system nearly 5 billion years ago. Encrusted with ices from the gas that made up the cloud from which the sun formed, they are in wide-swinging orbits of the sun. Sometimes going away as far as ten times the distance of the outermost planet, comets swing back close to the sun. Radiation from the sun blows away the ice in the same way that wind blows fresh snow from the roof of a moving car. Sometimes comets break up and spread fragments all around the stretched elliptical ring that forms their orbit. Earth plows through this debris on its own orbit of the sun. This produces meteor showers in earth's atmosphere.

Halley's Comet last appeared in early 1986 and will appear again in 76 years. Each time it gets a little less bright than the previous occasion when it passed close to the sun.

The sun will die one day and expand to envelop the earth.

All stars go through a life cycle fixed by their size and temperature. Stars are born in clouds of gas and dust, collapsing into nuclear reactors producing enormous amounts of energy in the form of radiation, heat, and light. When nuclear reactions cease, the clouds begin to collapse again. Before this happens, some stars puff themselves up to many times their former size. Our sun is just another star. In something less than 5 billion years from now, it will become a *red giant.* A red giant is what astronomers call a star close to the end of its life. The outer shell expands and the star grows to several times its stable size. The size depends on the original size of the star. In the case of our sun, its outer shell will grow to envelop the earth, now 93 million miles from the surface of the sun. All life will be destroyed long before that as the temperatures increase. When the sun reaches its climax, even the earth will be destroyed.

Many billions of years from now, the sun will expand into what astronomers call a red giant, puffing itself up to envelop the earth in its orbit.

Solar storms on the sun generate more energy than the earth has used since time began.

Every second the sun pours out 4 million tons of energy. The core of the sun where nuclear reactions take place has a temperature of 15 million degrees, but the surface is only 6,000 degrees. The surface is called the *photosphere* and often has sunspots that grow for several days before disappearing. Sunspots are linked to solar storms that erupt with little warning. Every eleven years, storms and sunspots reach peak intensity and send violent waves of matter through the solar system. Solar flares are giant loops of matter with enormous amounts of energy. Some are more than 300,000 miles high above the surface of the sun. Satellites watch for solar storm activity. Flares can seriously disrupt communications. It is not uncommon for one flare to erupt, releasing more energy than humans have used since they first appeared on Earth. But one word of warning: never, ever, look at the sun through a telescope. It will leave you totally blind — forever.

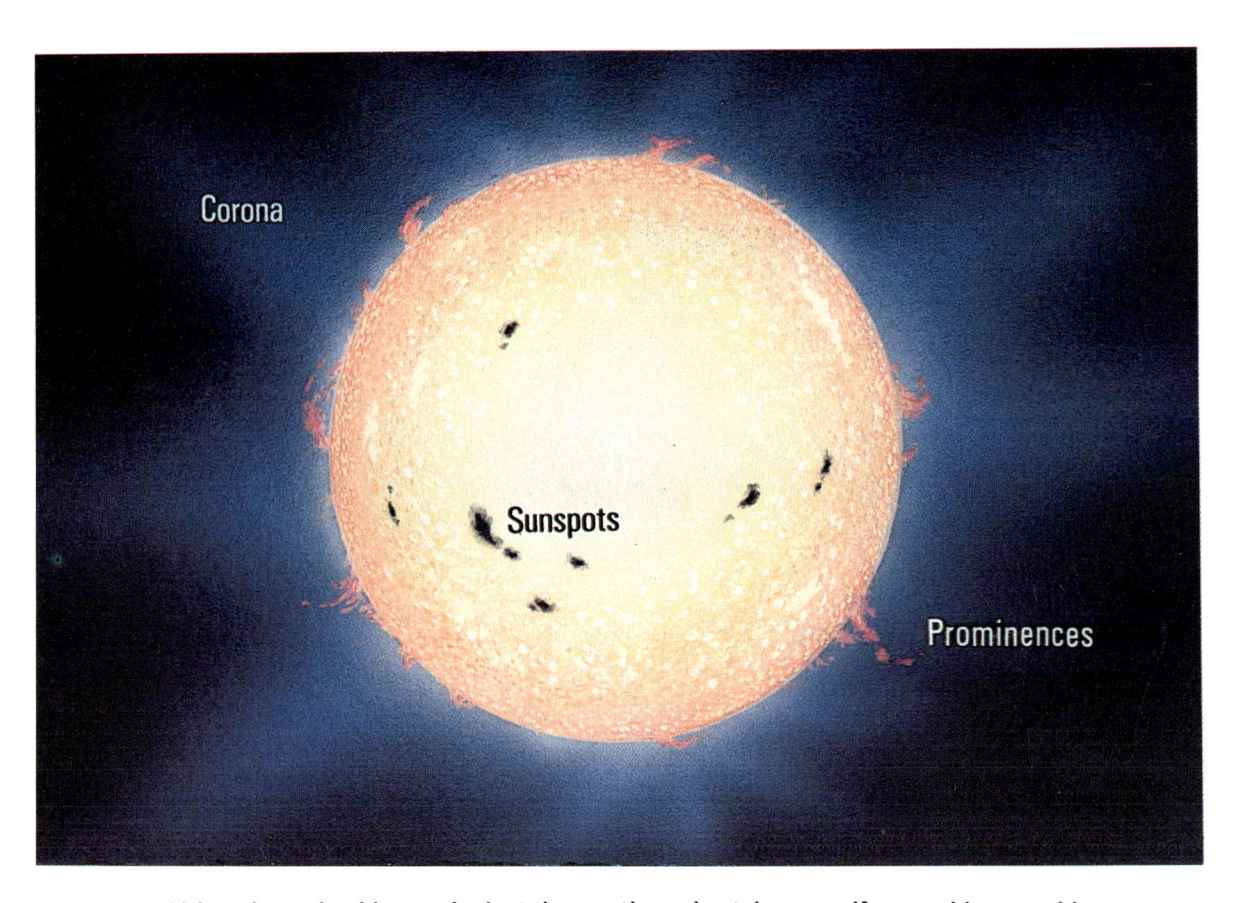

Although we should never look at the sun through a telescope, if we could we would see many sunspots and flares, called prominences, erupting into what scientists call the corona, its outer atmosphere.

Our sun is nearly 5 billion years old.

The sun around which the earth, eight other planets, the moon, and all the comets revolve is nearly 5,000 million years old. It began, as did all the other matter in the solar system, when a blast wave from nearby exploding stars crushed gas and rocky debris together, turning the middle into a nuclear reactor. This happens because nuclear reactions start at a temperature of about 15 million degrees under great pressure. The reactor became the sun and has been shining steadily ever since. In its core, more than 4 million tons of energy is being released every second. Without this there could have been no life on Earth. Will the sun ever die? Yes. Astronomers think that the sun will reach the end of its life in about another 5,000 million years, give or take a few hundred million years or so!

Left: Stars begin when huge explosions compress large amounts of gas and dust in a nebula, like this seen in the constellation Orion.

Right: Lagoon Nebula lies in the constellation Sagittarius and contains many young, hot stars just forming into new suns.

The only natural starlight comes from nuclear reactions.

Light was the first thing that appeared when the universe was created billions of years ago. Light comes from nuclear explosions all over the universe. These explosions are not manmade bombs, but natural events. Stars shine from energy released deep in their cores along with radiation and heat. All the *elements* that exist in the universe today are manufactured in these nuclear reactors. In the beginning, only hydrogen and a little helium existed. Stars gradually produced heavier elements, such as oxygen, carbon, and iron, by joining together, or fusing, atoms in the nuclear reaction. When stars reach the end of their lives, they frequently explode, blowing themselves to pieces. The elements are not destroyed but returned back into space to make up new stars, new planets, and perhaps even new people. All the atoms that make up our bodies were fused in the core of some now-dead star.

Natural starlight comes from nuclear reactions occurring right at the core of stars like our sun.

A star shines for billions of years without fuel.

When a fire burns, it consumes fuel. That fuel might be wood, paper, plastic, or anything else that burns. Stars do not burn, but they pour out enormous amounts of heat and light for thousands of millions of years just the same. They are not consumed in the process, because stars are giant nuclear reactors *making* elements rather than destroying materials. Stars are made up of atoms from which elements are made. A star shines because its core is very hot, often more than 15 million degrees. A considerable amount of agitation exists, and hydrogen atoms smash together and weld themselves into bigger atoms. This changes the element from hydrogen to helium, and then on to heavier and heavier elements. In this process, millions of tons of energy is released each second. Some stars are hot and small, while others are cool and big. All stars have a beginning and an end. Some last a few hundred million years, and others endure for billions of years.

Nuclear reactions are production lines for heavy elements in the universe, producing all the materials that make up the planets and everything on Earth.

You can see only 3,000 stars with the naked eye.

Have you ever looked out on a clear moonless night and counted the stars? You would be counting forever, you say. Not so. There are only about 3,000 stars visible to the naked eye.

Stars are big suns far away in space, shining billions of miles. Pockets of dust and gas hide stars farther away and block out their light. In addition, light does not continue at its same strength for ever. Scientists say light falls off on the *inverse square law.* Light that is twice as far away is only one-fourth as strong. Light five times away is only one-twenty fifth as strong. The average person's eyes can collect light from about 3,000 stars in the southern sky. But you would have to travel south of the equator to see those extra 3,000. To see more, you need a telescope to gather extra light.

Altogether, in both the northern and southern hemispheres, the naked eye can see a total 6,000 stars, but only 3,000 at any one time.

Our sun is just one of billions of stars in the galaxy.

The average person can see 3,000 stars in the northern hemisphere and 3,000 stars in the southern hemisphere. All but one belong to our galaxy, a vast colony of 200,000 million stars in a flattened disc like a dinner plate, bulging at the middle. The one exception is another galaxy called Andromeda. It is more than 2 million light years away. Our galaxy is called the Milky Way and is about 200,000 light years across. It has spiral arms of gas and dust radiating from the center. Our sun and its planets lie 30,000 light years out from the center and 20,000 light years from the edge. The solar system moves around the center of the galaxy, just like the planets go around the sun. To circle the galaxy even once takes more than 200 million years — and that's traveling at a speed of nearly 600,000 MPH! In all the universe, astronomers believe there may be millions of millions of galaxies like our Milky Way.

Left: One of the most dramatic sights in the sky is the Andromeda galaxy, more than 2 million light years from the Milky Way, our own galaxy.

Right: With the exception of Andromeda, which looks like a single point of light to the naked eye, every star we see in the sky belongs to our own Milky Way galaxy.

A black hole might be a tunnel to other worlds.

Albert Einstein was a great mathematician. At the beginning of this century, he wrote laws about the universe. Since then scientists have proved many of the things Einstein said. One of the more astonishing things about the universe is that it might have millions of black holes. Black holes are believed to be collapsed stars so massive they shrink down under their own gravity into nothing. Everything about black holes fits with what astronomers see in the universe. The same mathematics that proves the possibility of a black hole says it is impossible for something to be crushed into nothing. The only way out is for black holes to lead to worm holes. Worm holes would link tunnels connecting a black hole to a white hole. Everything that goes into a black hole would come out through a white hole. Perhaps in a different place and time — perhaps in a different universe.

A giant star loses clouds of matter sucked into a black hole invisible to the naked eye because it emits no light.

A massive black hole might exist at the center of our galaxy.

All stars belong to galaxies, and the galaxy to which the sun and its nine planets belong is called the Milky Way. It contains more than 200 million stars, each about the size of our sun.

When stars die, they collapse down to a dense ball. Big stars more than twice the weight of the sun collapse into black holes. The black hole is predicted by mathematicians and astronomers, although no one has seen one. Nothing escapes, not even light. Theory has it that a black hole squeezes down into literally nothing. It gobbles matter that comes near it, getting bigger all the time. Some astronomers believe they have seen signs of a black hole at the center of our galaxy. Anything going near it would disappear, but black holes give themselves away by heating up space all around. This is what astronomers think they have seen.

Huge galaxies like this one in Ursa Major may contain several black holes. The Milky Way is thought to have one large black hole at its center.

The crab nebula is debris from an astronomical explosion.

When stars die, they puff themselves up to many times their former size — and then blow up. At least some do. Others just expand rapidly and then collapse. One star that blew up in what is called *supernova* is the Crab Nebula. The blow-up happened in 1054, but what we see really took place 3,500 years earlier. It takes 3,500 years for light to reach us. To people on Earth, it was a bright light in the night sky that quickly faded. Telescopes have unlocked its secrets for astronomers and scientists. When a star gets to the end of its life, nuclear reactions expand out from the core and the star becomes unstable. In a massive explosion that blows apart almost all the matter in the star, great waves of energy are released. The outer shells of the star explode outwards at more than 20 million MPH. What is left collapses down to a solid ball in the middle, called a neutron star. This is what lies at the center of the Crab Nebula.

Stars that explode and release most of their matter in gigantic explosions, like the Crab Nebula did, help put matter back into space. Other stars and planets will re-form from that matter.

You would grow 100 miles tall if you stood on the surface of a dead star.

When stars are born it is because gas and dust gather and are pushed into a ball, which begins to collapse but instead heats up and becomes a nuclear reactor. Nuclear reactions hold the star up against collapse in the same way that air keeps a balloon inflated. When stars die, it is because they have used up all the atoms they need to make nuclear reactions. As the star pours out less and less energy, gravity takes over and it begins to collapse. Big stars collapse further, because gravity increases with the weight of the object. So it is with stars. A star 10 million miles across would collapse to one a few thousand miles wide. It becomes extremely dense and pulls objects toward it at enormous speed. If you stood on the surface of a star about to collapse into a black hole your feet would be pulled many times faster than your head. In that final millionth of a second, you would stretch 100 miles tall.

When stars reach the end of their life, they collapse down into dense concentrations of matter, sometimes becoming what astronomers call neutron stars.

A telescope to be launched by the shuttle will let us see the beginning of the universe.

By looking out in space, we see back through time. This is because light travels at a fixed speed. Light takes one second to travel 186,200 miles. That is about 670 million MPH. It would take a beam of light 1.3 seconds to reach the moon from Earth. Sunlight reaches Earth in about 8 minutes; we see the sun as it was 8 minutes ago. In astronomy, light speed is a unit of distance measured in years. One light year is the distance light travels in that time, nearly 5,900 billion miles. An object 1,000 light years away is seen as it was 1,000 years ago, because light has taken that long to reach us. Because of distortions in the atmosphere, telescopes on Earth can only see so far. NASA will soon launch the Hubble Telescope into space. With it astronomers will see objects nearly 20 billion light years away. This means they are 20 billion years old. As old as the universe.

NASA plans to launch a giant orbiting space telescope. It will be able to see further into the depths of the universe than any other telescope yet built.

Time travel might be a real possibility.

For centuries people have wished they could travel through time, visiting people in the future or going back into the past. In recent years, scientists have come up with theories that might make time travel a reality. Early this century, Albert Einstein wrote scientific laws about travel at the speed of light. He said that time slows down as speed gets faster for the person on a space trip. For instance, if a man flies to the nearest star at close to the speed of light (186,200 miles a second), time will slow down for him. He might take five Earth years to get there and five Earth years to get back. The Earth and all its people will have aged ten years. Our space traveler will have aged only one or two years. To him, the trip will have lasted only two years at most. If our space traveler went on a trip that for him lasted 30 years, he might return to an Earth that is 5,000 years older. For him it would be a trip into the future. For people on Earth, he would be a visitor from the past.

Time travelers may one day leave Earth to go on thousand-year voyages into the deepest parts of the universe. When they return to Earth, they will be visitors from the past.

GLOSSARY

Apollo	The manned space program organized by NASA to support the landing of astronauts on the surface of the moon between 1969 and 1972.
Astronomer	The scientist who studies astronomy and usually uses telescopes to make observations of objects in space.
Electrophoresis	A means of using electric current to separate various elements from a fluid for the purpose of preparing and manufacturing drugs and medicines.
Elements	Any one of up to 105 known substances that consist of atoms with the same number of protons in the nucleus.
Infrared	The part of the electromagnetic spectrum with a longer wavelength than light but a shorter wavelength than radio waves. Like radio waves, infrared radiation cannot be seen with the unaided human eye.
Inverse Square Law	A sequence of opposite variations such that an increase in one results in a decrease in the other.
Lunar module	The spacecraft used to ferry astronauts from moon orbit down to the surface and back again during the Apollo program between 1969 and 1972.
Magnetism	The property of attraction displayed by magnets in which a field of force is caused by a moving electric charge.
Milky Way	The spread of stars across the sky that forms the central band of the galaxy of which the sun and its planets are a member.
Minerals	A class of naturally occurring dead substances with characteristic form and a uniform chemical composition.
NASA	National Aeronautics and Space Administration, set up in October, 1958 for the peaceful exploration of space.
Photosphere	The visible surface of the sun.
Red giant	A star close to the end of its life which, after expanding to many times its original size, changes from white or yellow to red.
Spectrum	The distribution of colors produced when white light is dispersed by a prism.
Supernova	The visible cloud of material formed when, near the end of its life, a star partly explodes and sheds most of its material.
Ultraviolet	The part of the electromagnetic spectrum with wavelengths shorter than light, invisible to the naked eye.
Vacuum	A state of empty space without air or any measurable quantity of gas.
Viking	The NASA unmanned robot spacecraft designed to search for life on the surface of Mars, launched in 1975 and successfully put down on Mars during 1976.

INDEX

Page numbers in *italics* refer to photographs or illustrations.

Apollo lunar module	*21*	NASA	8, 12, 14, 22, 44
Apollo moon rover	20		
Apollo spacecraft	16, *20*, 21	Neutron stars	*43*
Andromeda	*39*	Newton, Issac	7
		Nuclear power	18
Black holes	40, 41, 43	Nuclear reactions in space	33-37, 42, 43
Cape Canaveral	*9*	Orbiter	*9*
Communication satellites	*16*	Orion	*35*
Conrad, Pete	*10*		
Crab Nebula	42	Planets	25
Dipolar magnetism	17	Red giant	33
Earth	14, 17, 18, 20, 23-26, 29-33	Remanent magnetism	17
		Rocketdyne	6
Earth years	45	Sagittarius	*35*
Einstein, Albert	40, 45	Saturn	31
Europa	31	Saturn V rocket	6
Explorer 1	16	Shuttle	9, *11*, 12, 14, 44
		Skylab	10
F-1 rocket motor	6	Solar flares	*34*
		Solar power satellite	*18*
Galileo, the astronomer	19	Solar system, origin of	32
Goddard, Robert	6	Solid rocket booster	9
		Space station	8, *10*
Halley's Comet	*32*	Speed of light	44, 45
Hubble Telescope	44	Stars	33, 36-43
		Sun	33, 34, 35, 36
Infrared camera	*15*		
Inverse square law	38	Sunspots	*34*
		Supernova	42
Jupiter	31		
		Ursa Major	*41*
Lagoon Nebula	*35*		
Lunar module	20	Vacuum	7
Lunar roving vehicle	20	Venus	*30*
		Viking lander	*27*, 29
Magnetic field	17	Viking orbiter	28
Mars	8, 27, *28*, 29		
Meteor showers	32	Walker, Charles	*14*
Microwave beam	18	Weightlessness	10-14, 19
Milky Way	*39*, 41	White hole	40
Moon	8, 17, 19, 20-26, 31, 35		

47